THE CHURCH AND THE WAR

THE CHURCH
AND THE WAR

By

KARL BARTH

Translated By

ANTONIA H. FROENDT

With an Introduction By

SAMUEL McCREA CAVERT

WIPF & STOCK · Eugene, Oregon

Wipf and Stock Publishers
199 W 8th Ave, Suite 3
Eugene, OR 97401

The Church and The War
By Karl Barth
Copyright©1944 by Karl Barth
ISBN 13: 978-1-60608-026-9
Publication date 6/11/2008

© of the German original version
Theologischer Verlag Zürich, 1944

INTRODUCTION

IN CONNECTION with a visit to Switzerland in September and October, 1942, it was my good fortune to become acquainted with Karl Barth. I first saw him in Liestal, when he was in the uniform of a captain in the Swiss Army, completing a period of active military service. The next day, while sitting at tea with him in Basle—only a few miles from Nazi fortifications—in the home of Pastor A. Koechlin, President of the Swiss Church Federation, I discovered that the Swiss theologian was intensely interested in knowing what American Christians were thinking about the international situation. When the conversation turned to his own convictions about the war, and particularly to views which he had expressed in a letter to British Christians published a year earlier, I suggested that he write a letter of similar character to Christians of the United States.

Dr. Barth's first reaction to the suggestion was decidedly negative. He feared that he would appear intrusive and presumptuous if, never having been in America, he should undertake to give advice to American Christians. He also felt that he had too little knowledge both of America and of American Christianity to be able to say anything of value or even of interest to us. Ten days later, however, when we were both in Geneva as guests of W. A. Visser 't Hooft, General Secretary of the Provisional Committee of the World Council of Churches, I reopened the question. Dr. 't Hooft reinforced my plea that a friendly communication from Dr. Barth to American Christians would help to build up ecumenical understanding. We urged that Dr. Barth's great service to the entire Church by his prophetic and courageous opposition to National Socialism in its earlier days had placed all Christians in his debt and meant that his words would receive an eager welcome. He finally agreed that if I would formulate certain questions in which American Christians are especially interested he would answer them frankly.

The reader should bear in mind that the Letter to American Christians is only a partial exposition of Dr. Barth's views. It is the latest in a series of similar letters addressed to Christians in several countries. In 1938, at the time of the Munich crisis, he wrote to the Czech Christians, praising their resistance and declaring that in fighting for the "righteous state" they were also indirectly fighting for the Church of Christ. In 1939 he wrote a Letter to the French Protestants, shortly before the collapse of the Republic. In 1940 he wrote again to the French Protestants, while they were in an agony of suffering after the Nazi triumph. A letter to the British Christians was penned in April, 1941, after the repulse of the attempted Nazi invasion. The French and the British letters have been published under the title "This Christian Cause."

Each of these letters, including the American, is an *ad hoc* document, addressed to a particular group of Christians in particular historical circumstances. A more formal and systematic interpretation of Dr. Barth's position *vis à vis* the war is given in his little book, "The Church and the Political Problem of Our Day." In it he sets forth his conception of both the State and the Church. Over against this he interprets National Socialism as at once "the radical dissolution of the just State" and also a pseudo-religious institution of salvation "fundamentally hostile to Christianity."

Dr. Barth's service in exposing the anti-Christian character of National Socialism is too little known in America. It was his teaching in Germany in the decade before Hitler's rise to power that paved the way for the resistance that took form in the Confessional Church. The Confessional Church was not a new Church but a group within the German Church that "confessed" with fresh insight and devotion, relevant to the immediate political situation, the historic statements of faith associated with the Reformation. In 1934, the year after Hitler's consolidation of power in Germany, a conference of the Confessional group, held at Barmen, drew up the short declaration of six points which became a great rallying-ground for opposition to Nazism in the Church. Dr. Barth was more responsible than any other person for the Barmen declaration. Its keynote is that "Jesus Christ, as He is witnessed to in the Scriptures, is the Word of God which we have to hear, which we have to trust and give heed to." This was the theological basis for rejecting the Nazi "revelations" of blood and soil and denying that a Christian's final loyalty could be given to an earthly *fuehrer*.

The extent to which the heroic stand of Christians in Germany, Czecho-Slovakia, Norway, Holland, and several other countries has been due to Karl Barth no one can estimate with confidence, but certainly his teaching and testimony were a most timely and potent force. The Nazis knew what they were doing when they forced him out of his university post in the year following the Barmen Synod and compelled him to seek refuge in his native Switzerland! Probably history will record that his influence was one of the great preservers of Christianity in Europe's crisis.

Implicit in the Letter to American Christians are important theological assumptions. Perhaps it may be helpful if they are more explicitly indicated. At the risk of failing to do justice to Dr. Barth, I venture to give a very condensed summary of some of his convictions.

1. Jesus Christ is Lord of the whole creation, manifested as such in His resurrection, which is the evidence that all power has been given to Him in heaven and on earth. It is this ultimate Kingly authority of Jesus Christ—not any con-

sideration derived from "natural law" or the value of personality or social ethics—which is the foundation-stone of Dr. Barth's thinking about the relation of the Church and the Christian to National Socialism and the war.

2. The Lordship of Christ cannot be limited to what is sometimes called the "inner life." His Kingly Rule extends not only over the Church but over the entire life of mankind, confronting the "principalities and powers of this world." The realm of politics, therefore, is not exempt from His sway.

3. The sole function of the Church is to preach the Word of God and bear witness to the Lordship of Christ. This involves, of course, the definite confession of Him as "the One who has come to us as Son of God and Saviour and will come again"; it also involves "the *actualizing* of this confession in definite decisions" with reference to contemporary problems. In order to "actualize" her confession the Church must preach the Word of God, not *in vacuo* but in terms that are clearly relevant to men in the concrete historical circumstances in which they are placed. To bear faithful witness to Christ must bring the Church into a relationship to questions which are agitating both Christians and the world "here and now at the present moment."

4. The State, as well as the Church, has its own important and indispensable place in the Divine economy. Part of the Lordship of Christ is exercised through the "righteous" (or "just") State, whose function is to maintain order and justice as against the chaos and injustice to which man's sinful nature makes him prone. The State would fail in its duty as "an appointed minister of God" if it failed to defend right against wrong—if necessary, by the use of force.

5. It is the duty of Christians to help establish and preserve the just State. National Socialism, it cannot be too strongly insisted, is a "fundamental dissolution of the just State." The Church must therefore say "No" to it—a "No" as unequivocal as the "No" to any other flagrant evil, like alcoholism or prostitution. Faith in the sovereignty of Jesus Christ and assent to the sovereignty of National Socialism are mutually

exclusive. Hence the Christian is doing the will of God in opposing the Nazi conquest.

This does not mean that Dr. Barth conceives the war against National Socialism either as a crusade or as a means of furthering the Kingdom of God. It is rather "a large-scale police measure" for repulsing nihilism and anarchism. As such, he holds, it is something which Christians who understand the nature of National Socialism, in contrast with the true nature of the State, must support.

The superficial impression, rather widely held in America, that Dr. Barth is unsocial and "other-worldly" in his conception of Christianity can hardly survive a careful perusal of his Letter to American Christians, or his other writings about the war.

Dr. Barth wrote his Letter of American Christians" in December, 1942. Due to difficulties in communication with Switzerland after the occupation of Southern France, the Letter was long delayed in reaching this country. It is possible that some of his views (for example, about the role of the Church after the war) might be somewhat modified if he were writing the Letter today.

The questions to which Dr. Barth addresses himself in the Letter to American Christians fall into two groups: first, those having to do with the proper function of the Church in relation to the war; second, those that deal with the responsibility of the Church in post-war reconstruction. The two subjects are here treated in separate chapters (II and III) although in his original manuscript they constituted a single document.

Chapter I, while of a different character, is closely related in spirit and outlook to the Letter to American Christians, and, like the Letter, was written especially for American readers. It is a careful review of the way in which the Protestant churches of Europe had met the crisis of National Socialism and the war up to the Fall of 1942. This statement is of front-rank historical importance and is also significant for its indirect disclosure of Dr. Barth's judgments on the elements of strength and of weakness in the churches of Europe.

Most of Chapter I appeared in *Foreign Affairs,* January, 1943. Parts of Chapters II and III appeared in *Christendom,* Fall Issue, 1943. The courtesy of the editors of these two quarterly journals in permitting the reprinting of their articles is warmly appreciated.

SAMUEL MCCREA CAVERT

CONTENTS

xi

CHAPTER I

The Churches of Europe in the Face of the War

WHAT have the Protestant churches of Europe learned, suffered and achieved in the world crisis? What may be expected —for them, and from them—in the days to come?

I

The present world crisis began when the National Socialists came to power in Germany in the year 1933. It found most of the Protestant Churches of Europe in the initial stages of a process of internal and external rebuilding and consolidation on the basis of a renewed consciousness of their peculiar nature and mission.

The catastrophe of the World War of 1914–1918 was widely felt to have been a serious indictment of the Church and of the Christianity of that day, still strongly under the influence of the intellectual and political developments of the eighteenth and nineteenth centuries. Not only shallow detractors held this conviction, but also many enlightened exponents of the Protestant tradition and mission. The effect, however, had not been to produce discouragement but rather to lead many to ask themselves, with new emphasis, the question: What is the basic principle and function of the Church in a human society which obviously is sick almost to death? As was the case during the Renaissance, the return to the Church's historic origins played a decisive role in the posing and answering of this question. It did not produce either

1

a new religious philosophy and orientation or a new program of religious activity, but it did lead to a rediscovery of the unique content of the Bible and of the significance of the Reformation era and the still older Church—a rediscovery which all of us would have thought most unlikely before the present catastrophe.

The diluted bourgeois religion and ethics of the early twentieth century became "the dead past" while the message of the Old and New Testament, as we found it for the most part rightly interpreted by Luther and Calvin, became "the living present." We did not become orthodox ("fundamentalist") in the sense of the repetition of some historical dogmas, but we tried, freely and in our own present-day way, to think again biblically and evangelically and to give back to the preaching and life of our churches their biblical and evangelical Protestant conformation. This conformation they had pretty well lost at the time of the First World War, so that actually they were no longer that "salt of the earth" which they should and could be. We felt obliged to restore to its rightful position the elements of objective truth which must ever be the secret of a living Church and which must be given recognition if the Church is to be differentiated from an inspirational conventicle and if its message is to have meaning for the life and living of human beings.

I say "we," for I am thinking of a whole generation of responsible persons in all the Protestant churches of Europe. Partly in agreement with each other, partly without such agreement or even in opposition to one another, without organization of any kind but nevertheless in an unmistakable objective solidarity, we entered upon this way. I note explicitly that the so-called "dialectic theology," often associated with my name, was only one phenomenon among others. There were, and are, many and various ways to walk on this road.

Protest and reaction of all sorts made themselves felt, and, of course, unintelligent and undesirable henchmen were not lacking. Above all, indifference was for a time invincible. It

2

is nevertheless true to say that, by and large, this beginning of an inward renewal springing from the living foundations of the Church of Jesus Christ was the answer given by European Protestantism to the question posed by the First World War. The majority of our theological students and of young men interested in things Christian began to seek progress along these lines.

Theology necessarily had to give recognition, favorable or critical, to this transformation. Roman Catholicism and contemporary philosophy took notice of it as they had never previously noticed developments within Protestantism. A Berlin churchman who tried to claim that the twentieth century was the "century of the Church" was, of course, going too far. But it remains a fact that interest in and understanding of Protestant ecclesiastical doctrine and order increased in comparison to what they had been in the second half of the nineteenth century, often in unexpected ways and places. For example, the prestige of the Protestant churches, and to a certain extent their popularity also, grew in government circles in a number of countries. And a certain wholesome Christian self-consciousness again became a fact in Europe.

True enough, it was only a beginning. Many of the new positions were (and still remain) unclarified, vulnerable and even self-contradictory. There were too many problems to be mastered or even surveyed in the course of a few years. It was too much to hope that the Protestant peoples would be permeated by the new conception at once, that prejudices and misunderstandings firmly rooted for centuries among both the educated and the uneducated could be removed immediately. We must be under no self-deception concerning the tentative character of the preliminary gains, especially in those countries where the transformation appeared most spontaneously and vigorously—Germany, Holland and Switzerland. In France, in Scandinavia, among the Hungarian and Italian Protestants, only relatively small groups had begun to work. Fifteen years after the First World War, all those who were seriously participating in the movement and

3

were well-informed about it were aware that the time had come to start really intensive and extensive work.

The Protestant churches in Europe, then, were not wholly unprepared when the first shocks of the earthquake came in 1933, heralding the world catastrophe of today. In so far as the churches had participated in the renewal of which I have spoken, they had, after all, at least a slight start on the Nazi. It is hard to say what would have become of them if it had not been for this, if the sudden assault of 1933 had found them as they were, for example, in 1910.

II

It must not be forgotten that opposition to the anti-Semitic, aggressive, totalitarian, national state was not at first so general as it has become since the outbreak of the present war. At the outset, the attitude of "Western Civilization" to that state was not certain. It is not fair to accuse the German intellectuals and the German Democrats and Social Democrats of weakness and disloyalty without mentioning the many Frenchmen, Englishmen and Americans who allowed themselves to be deceived at a distance just as those nearer by were deceived. As late as 1938, some of these foreigners permitted themselves to be received as honored guests in Berlin, and recorded a reverential and even somewhat envious admiration of what they saw there.

For a time it was uncertain whether one might not see in Hitler's spirit, method and enterprise something like an apotheosis of the movement of emancipation which began with the Renaissance. Was not this the true face of the absolutely self-sufficient man, who had long since become the ideal not only of Germans but of all modern culture as it is related to economic and technical progress? If human affairs could develop as logically as they do in theory, it might easily have happened that not only Germany and Europe, but the entire modern world, apparently long detached from its Christian roots, would have welcomed the Hitlerian system

4

as the kingdom of the superman toward which it had always secretly aspired.

After all, even in his utterly insane reconstruction of history, Hitler is not entirely wrong when he keeps referring to the Jew as the obstacle which has thus far prevented this logical development of events. The existence of the Jew probably is the symbol of the objective metaphysical fact, independent of all intellectual counter-movements, that the Christian root of Western culture is still alive. Without credit to him, and even against his will, the Jew is witness to the continuing vitality of the Old and New Testament revelation, by virtue of which Western culture, despite the degree of its present and possible future apostasy, is separated as by an abyss from the inherent Godlessness of National Socialism. This revelation can be misconstrued, but never wholly overlooked or forgotten. Hitler knows what he wants better than he may be aware when he selects the Jew as the world's Public Enemy No. 1. Wherever the Christian revelation, whose actual witness is the Jew, is recognized and understood, the struggle against National Socialism ceases to be accidental and superficial and becomes fundamental and essential.

Western civilization failed to confront National Socialism firmly because the realization of the Christian revelation among the civilized people of the West (not only among the Germans!) had become dim. Men did not see the inherent atheism of the Hitlerian system. Hence, they could not be sure whether the antithesis between a legitimate state and a robber state, between democracy and absolute dictatorship, might not simply be a difference in taste, evaluation or political technique. Thinking in that way, how could people have been capable of a serene faith in Western culture and of firm resistance to that which threatened it? How could they think otherwise than they did, blind and deaf as they had become to the revelation of the Old and New Testament?

There was resistance to Hitler from the very first on the

part of those who were on their way back to a conscious realization of the Christian presupposition of Western culture. In these circles it was not easy to mistake a human authority, however powerful, for that of God; a community of "race, blood and soil" for the Communion of Saints; the might of brutality for the power of truth. This group could not accept or treat the Jewish problem as a "racial question." The first serious protest against Hitlerism necessarily had to come, and did in fact come, from the ranks of the Protestant churches that had been touched by the "renewal." They were the first to grasp the essential impossibility of the totalitarian state, the negation of life inherent in the Hitlerian doctrine of unfreedom, the impudent denial of the intellect by the National Socialist cult of physical force. They saw through the intolerable implication of the neo-German anti-Semitism. Inevitably, it was in this quarter that alert and resolute wardens were found for Western culture, for freedom of conscience and speech, for the democratic state.

III

It was inevitable that the Christian "substance" of the churches should prove intolerable to National Socialism. Rauschning was right when he defined the actual content of National Socialism as pure, logical and therefore wholly destructive and anti-spiritual nihilism. In no other way is it possible to explain either the peculiar character of its leading personalities, the inherently inhuman nature of all its modes of behavior or the demonically fascinating influence which emanates from it. It is easy to see where such a system might expect to find its most dangerous enemy. From the outset, its religious policy could only be directed toward the extirpation of the Christian faith and creed.

This goal, however, like other goals of National Socialism, could be approached only step by step, indirectly and under all sorts of disguises. In its naked form, National Socialism is a secret cult which is probably proclaimed openly only in the cloister-like training camps of the *élite*. Outside of this group were those educated or half-educated persons who were estranged from the Church but who still required a certain religiosity and religious ideology. They were offered a "German Faith," based on the old German paganism. In this cult the mystical personage "Germany" took the place of the Godhead, Führer Adolf Hitler became the prophet, and the church services were replaced by more or less appropriate rites exalting the German national character. There was never any seriously intended religious movement back of this neo-paganism which attracted so much attention in other countries. Like many other things in the Third Reich, it was "window-dressing" for overgrown children; but as such it has been by no means ineffective.

This is even more true of the artificial structure of a "German Christianity" which was presented to those parts of the population which were more or less actively interested in the Church. According to this concept, National Socialism was to be the real "positive Christianity," in contrast to Judaism and Bolshevism, which were regarded as the embodiments of everything heathen. It was to be a new revelation from God, but one that was identical with that in Jesus Christ, or at least closely related to it! After all, it had been possible in the past to bring into a similar positive relationship to Christianity the bourgeois moralism of rationalism, later the idealistic philosophy of Goethe, then the monarchical nationalism of Bismarck's day, and still later Marxian Socialism. Why should not the same attempt be made with the Hitler system, which the nation believed was its hope of salvation? It was this fantastic but at the same time cogent proposition with which the Protestant churches had to deal.

The basic question was: Had comprehension of the unique character and independence of the Christian Gospel completely died out, or had it reawakened, and, if so, what would be the reaction to the particular new temptation of 1933? The answer to this question is found in the fact that while the German political parties, German jurisprudence, science,

7

art and philosophy capitulated, the churches formed the first opposition to the current which was sweeping all before it.

Out of the conflict against the National Socialist version of Christianity there arose, under the leadership of Martin Niemöller, first the "Pastors' *Notbund*" (Emergency Union), and then, on a wider base, the "Confessional Church" (*Bekennende Kirche*). They attempted quite simply to defend the basic essentials of Christianity, the preaching of the Word and the order of the Church, against the strange new faith which was being imposed on them but which they could not accept as Christian. This gave their movement an essentially conservative character. That, we see now, was their limitation: they concentrated solely on one specific phase of Nazi religious and church policy.

The pagan "German Faith" barely touched the edges of their field of vision, and the political problem of National Socialism did not come into it at all. This may be hard to understand, but it is necessary to realize that the fight of the Confessional Church was not directed against National Socialism as such. The latter's innate hostility to all things spiritual, as well as its anti-Christian tendency, were at that time only too successfully camouflaged. Most of the adherents of the Confessional Church, in fact, thought they could agree to, or at least sympathize with, the political and social aims of National Socialism. Their struggle was confined to the specific question whether the Church could remain the Church, i. e., could preach the Gospel according to the Old and New Testaments, or should be coördinated with the new political doctrine and combine its mission with it. Up to the year 1934, while I was in Germany, I myself thought that I could relegate my political opposition to the background and work only along that line.

Those who refuse to give the Confessional Church credit for its achievement in this narrow sector fail to realize how necessary it was to answer clearly the fundamental question just posed, how difficult it was at that time in Germany to

8

venture to contradict the official answer to that question, and how loyally and energetically the battle has been fought to this day by thousands of known and unknown men and women. If an indictment were to be brought against them, it would not be that they began along these lines, but that they did not go on from there. They took their stand on behalf of the Jewish Christians, for the freedom and purity of the Christian creed and worship, for suitable theological training and for a parish life built around a sincere study of the Bible. But they were not able (alas, in many cases they did not even really want!) to prevent the rise of National Socialism in Germany with its malignant development into a menace to all the rest of the world. Nonetheless, they helped to cross Hitler's purpose at a very decisive point by making it possible for free Protestant Christianity, despite all the cunning assaults against it, to survive in Germany and retain its power of germination.

Not merely did the German Christians not "conquer" the churches, as they had made up their minds to do in 1933, but they were ignominiously dropped by the National Socialists when they failed to accomplish their purpose. In this one field the National Socialist system met a force which it was able to suppress but not to break. To that extent the Confessional Church was the vanguard of the more comprehensive resistance which is being offered to Hitlerism today. Do not forget that this Church took its stand—within its limitations —when the tragedy of Munich and the subsequent slow awakening of most of the world to resistance still lay far in the future. The fate prepared for Martin Niemöller—he is still in the concentration camp of Dachau—by the personal order of the Führer, shows that the basic importance of the Confessional Church's resistance was fully recognized by the other side. Numerous other equally determined individuals are in concentration camps or have had to pay for their devotion to the cause with long prison sentences or even with their lives. Whatever one may think about their limitations of vision and aspiration, it is only right to remember them with special reverence among the many victims of the present crisis.

IV

The significance of the German Church's struggle was understood well enough by the other Protestant churches of Europe. It was more than the drama of what was unfolding near by, a drama in which a church was acting and suffering according to its best knowledge and conscience, that awakened sympathy in Holland, Switzerland, Scandinavia, France (and for a long time, also, among the Protestant Hungarians and Italians). There was also a realization that the common cause of the Gospel, now facing an obvious threat, was at stake in the stand taken by the Confessional Church. Communication between the churches was kept up as long as possible; Switzerland, especially, gave the Confessional Church in Germany a considerable amount of aid. A certain misunderstanding played a useful part in this from the beginning, the action of the German Confessional Church being interpreted in other countries as more broadly based and more radical than it really was.

The moment came soon enough when a number of these other churches were compelled by the German occupation of their respective countries to take their own stand on the problem first presented in Germany. The conflicts which broke out in Holland and Norway should be especially recalled.

Clearly there was a difference between the situation of the churches in those two countries and that of the Confessional Church in Germany. It is only fair to note three things:

1. The churches in Holland and Norway have the immeasurable advantage of defending not only the freedom of the Gospel, but the freedom of their own people and fatherland against foreign oppressors and traitors within their gates; the men of the German Confessional Church, on the other hand, have to stand up against their own government and are constantly faced by the

problem (which the war has made still more insistent) of reconciling their opposition to National Socialism with their duty and love for their own land and people.

2. The churches of Holland and Norway, before they themselves became part of the conflict, were able to learn much from their long observation of events in Germany; they could carry on their struggle in the light of the German experience.

3. The German occupation authorities, after the experience in Germany, did not meddle with the inner life of the churches in Holland and Norway or try to impose on them a pagan or heretical doctrine and order; as a result, these churches were able from the start to orient themselves more freely.

For these reasons the church struggle in Holland and Norway is a far more animated picture than in Germany. It takes for granted the answer to the question concerning the preservation of the Christian substance and is able to concentrate on the practical accomplishment of that aim. The fight is carried on and supported not merely by a minority but by an overwhelming majority of theologians and church members. It has a direct relationship to the struggle in which the nations, as such, are engaged. It is being waged not only on the defensive, but on the offensive as well. The issue is not merely the rights of the Church, but also the restoration of the general state of civil law destroyed by the German invasion; not faith alone is at stake, but the belief in the validity of God's commandments; it is not just a question of the Jewish Christians, but of the Jews in general. Even in the eyes of the individual who is only superficially, if at all, interested in Christian affairs, this struggle is now an important part of the general battle against National Socialism.

If the scope and significance of the church struggles in Holland and Norway are greater than those of the struggle in Germany, we must not overlook the fact that their Christian purity and depth and their relation to the religious "renewal" are perhaps more problematical. Motives and principles other than those which are purely Christian may play no small part here, and all sorts of naïve confusions may result —confusion between the cause of God and the national cause,

11

between hope in God and hope in the British; between a holy, prophetic wrath and the comprehensible but less holy rage of the oppressed and betrayed. The problem of the Prophet Jeremiah should be food for thought to the more serious Christian in Holland and Norway. It is undeniable that the church struggle in Germany is closely linked with the "renewal"; but it is at least uncertain whether the "renewal" is so much in the foreground of the vigorous action in which the Dutch and Norwegian Christians are at present engaged. Later we shall see which Church will emerge with the greatest spiritual gain from the developments of these days.

This reservation, however, does not alter the fact that the logical conclusion of the struggle begun in Germany itself would be the decisive political witness and devotion to God now apparent in these other countries. It is precisely because of the Christian belief in the resurrection of Christ from the dead, the faith that to Him is given all power in heaven and earth, that one cannot say to German National Socialism either "Yes" or "Yes and No," but only wholeheartedly and with complete decisiveness: "No!" Those who do otherwise have either failed to understand National Socialism, despite all its self-revelations; or they have not thought through the message of the Bible; or they have developed a kind of schizophrenia in which totally divergent yardsticks are adopted for the inner and the external life. One wonders uneasily whether even the sincere Christians in Germany have not become victims of that sort of intellectual disintegration. But no matter how far they may have progressed in other directions, they will have to learn from the other churches that there are a Christian center and a Christian periphery, that the Christian substance and its political application are indeed two different things, but that there is only one truth and one righteousness—and no man can serve two masters.

I know little or nothing about the present ecclesiastical situation in Denmark or among Protestants in Hungary,

Italy and the part of France which has been under German occupation since the Armistice. In the light of their antecedents, and also from certain direct indications, it is to be feared that the Hungarians, for whom we formerly had good hopes, have rather lost their heads as a result of their alliance with Germany and the war with Russia and now expect to find their Christian happiness in unrestrained anti-Bolshevism. The situation in occupied France appears to be similar to that in Germany, in that the French Church leaders, inwardly in passionate opposition to the German occupation, have been concentrating their attention on the inward life of the Church and on education of the community for a better future.

On the other hand, what has been said about Holland and Norway is applicable also to Switzerland, Sweden and the part of France until recently not directly under the Germans.

Reformed Switzerland, of course, has not yet been put to the test of actual war. But their country's isolated position in the midst of the Axis Powers has forced the Swiss urgently (though tentatively) to decide for or against the "New Order" in Europe. It is safe to say that Switzerland in general has answered with a unanimous negative, not through the mouth of the Swiss government, but by the voices of the preachers and the parishes (inclusive of Catholic Switzerland). During the First World War there was a not insignificant amount of Swiss anti-militarism; today the overwhelming majority of the Christian Swiss realize clearly that "obedience to constituted authority" (according to the thirteenth chapter of Romans), in the form of armed neutrality, is both righteous and necessary. The interpretation of the concept of Swiss neutrality has, however, caused sharp differences of opinion in several instances between certain church spokesmen and the federal authorities. The Swiss Church cannot be accused of having been silent when the government applied neutrality in a matter which was highly questionable alike from the Christian, the traditional and the prevailing legal viewpoint of our country. Nor can it be said that the Church failed to

13

act in a practical way in the matter of the foreign refugees, or that its general attitude has been wholly without impressiveness and effect. But, of course, our resistance can hardly be compared with that of the churches in Holland, Norway and (in a different manner) Germany.

News from Sweden indicates that, subject to similar conditions and reservations, the Swedish Church too belongs thus far not only to the Protestant but to the *protesting* churches.

Although the paralysis of the summer of 1940 at first led Protestantism in unoccupied France to withdraw into political quietism and the cultivation of piety and morals, a change seems to have occurred in 1941 and 1942. The principles and practices of the Vichy government and its relations with the foreign power which stood behind and over it were under constant debate. The vigorous action of the church leader, Pastor Marc Boegner, on behalf of the Christian education of youth, his courageous address to Marshal Pétain on the persecution of the Jews, and other news which has seeped out regarding the attitude and activity of the younger generation of pastors appear to indicate further developments along these lines whenever the occasion again offers.

What was said about the special danger inherent in the situation in Holland and Norway is to some extent true also of those churches which have not yet been directly attacked. We shall have to keep watch over the attitude they have taken, and also guard against impairing the freedom of the gospel in our zeal for the good and our aversion to evil, which in a reverse sense is just what National Socialism demanded of the German Church in the name of "German Christianity." And, above all, we shall have to be vigilant lest our courage and our enthusiasm for resistance become subject to the alternating political and military successes and setbacks. It must be clear that our resistance can have meaning and even political significance only to the extent that it is able to nourish itself from its own roots.

The thing that the Church must tell the world in the present crisis is this: that there is an *absolutely* essential antithesis to National Socialism which is independent of success or failure. But the Church can and will say this rightly only if it continues to go its own way.

V

Taking the situation as a whole, one may justly say that European Protestantism, with varying degrees of consistency, frankness and power, has recognized and assumed the position appropriate to its historic mission. It may be affirmed without presumption that it has sounded a clearer call than any which has as yet been heard from the Holy See in Rome, and that it need not be ashamed when measured against the other forces of resistance. We may be gratefully astonished that, hardly a hundred years after Kierkegaard's devastating criticism of Protestant Christianity, a vastly greater catastrophe than he visualized has not succeeded in overwhelming it.

But measured by the yardstick which has been in existence since the sixteenth century, and which we now take with new seriousness, the Protestant churches can find no occasion for satisfaction with the results of their efforts thus far. In the sixteenth century, Protestantism assumed a great responsibility for shaping the destiny of Europe. It has reason to ask itself, therefore, how it could happen that, after four hundred years, Europe could be brought to the uttermost edge of the abyss on which it stands today. And it is a monumental disgrace to all Protestantism that the monster of National Socialism could be born in the very cradle of the Reformation and could develop there into an object of dread and abomination to all the world.

It is part of the pattern of things that German theology, which up to the time of crisis gave guidance to the theologians of all the Protestant churches, should not have retained its leadership but instead should have become instrumental in leading men's souls astray. However, it is likewise part of the pattern of things that those of us who felt called

15

upon to take up the conflict either did so too late or did not know how to find the enkindling and potent word which would awaken the nations and prevent the approaching calamity—although it was clear enough that this word should be spoken and equally clear where it could be found. Furthermore, the Protestant churches, in Germany as well as in all the other countries, with the possible exception of Norway, did not possess the "watchmen" and leaders who might have known how to rouse them. They showed themselves on the whole to be ill-prepared to meet the problems of this time. The steps actually taken thus far have necessarily had a spasmodic, personal, voluntary and therefore often arbitrary origin and character. Even the ecumenical movement, although it increased in importance after the First World War, obviously had not yet developed far enough to furnish authoritative guidance to the churches or do more than provide a means for exchanging information.

Protestantism was altogether lacking in the intellectually consistent direction which it had enjoyed in the days of Calvin. For this reason, in the last analysis, the individual churches were left to themselves in their anxieties and problems and in their dangerous vacillation between quietism on the one hand and a secularizing activism on the other. The result was that the voice of Protestantism became the voice of one crying in the wilderness, or, more accurately, a voice coming out of a corner. Thus it was deprived of the power and effectiveness which it should have had, considering the mission entrusted to the churches of the Reformation. It is small consolation that the far better equipped Roman Catholic Church has done no better, in fact, not nearly so well. The fact is that probably we all have had too much of the weak and confused spirit of the eighteenth and nineteenth centuries to be equal to this crisis.

One can only speak theologically, not historically, of the reasons why we nevertheless were not altogether like sheep without a shepherd, and why it is possible to say, though with the greatest caution, that there is still an enduring Protestant

16

Church in Europe. The churches might well be compared, in the words of the Prophet, to a "brand snatched from the burning." One would have to admit that they can thank the inward renewal, to which reference has been made, for the little they have been able to achieve. The question of their future, immediate as well as remote, may well be decided, therefore, by whether this renewal continues vigorously, comes to a standstill or becomes in some way perverted.

The present crisis has evidently not yet reached its peak. The severest trials and tests of endurance for European Protestantism probably still lie ahead. And beyond the problems of wartime lie those of peace. "The old world is dead!" a leading English statesman has just proclaimed. He is probably right. Europe undoubtedly has come to the end of an historic, political, economic and social era and confronts an unexampled re-beginning. Equally true it is that its renewal must consist not in the destruction of Western culture, but in its unhindered efflorescence, rooted, as it is, in Christianity. The new life which is to follow the death of the old must be founded on this culture.

Will the confused and war-weary nations muster the courage, the insight and the will power to do this? Will they be able to comprehend that the world, for all its frailty and imperfection, after all the horror which it has known, still has a hope of better things? And will they comprehend further that without this hope no authentic quest for those better things will ever be attempted? It will be the function of the Christian churches to proclaim this hope and to make it comprehensible. That is going to be much harder than the essentially critical task of today, when we are still at war.

This hope is the great affirmation of the Gospel of Jesus Christ; but the churches will be able to proclaim and expound it to all peoples only if they themselves regain true knowledge of it and learn to live by it, only when they themselves are ready to move forward with simple, direct and complete faith in this Gospel. How shall they tell the world what they themselves no longer understand? Their whole weakness in the present crisis lies in the fact that they are only at the beginning of this return—or advance. They will be stronger in the future than they are in the present if their own process of renewal precedes the necessary and true renewal of Europe, if they do not stand still or deviate, but go forward.

There is no phase of European church life which does not stand in need of this renascence. The pastors must hear the call, but so must the congregations. Theology must listen to it, and also the church judicatories and the supporters of the ecumenical movement. There is no need to stress how much depends on whether or not they obey the call. If the old world is really dead, nothing less than the Gospel of the resurrection and the life must be preached and heard. This is the mission which will be entrusted to the Church tomorrow in a manner far different from that of yesterday.

But here again we are at the frontiers of a domain about which one can only speak theologically. The real renascence of the Church, as of Europe, does not ultimately lie in human hands. The Christian hope is the strongest hope of all the world, because it reaches immeasurably higher than the objectives which are attainable by political, economic, social or even ecclesiastical action. The Protestant churches will themselves look confidently into the future, and will awaken confidence in others, to the precise degree that they keep that hope before their eyes and are willing to accept it as *grace* and make it fruitful accordingly. If a further quickening is granted to them, and with it the insight and the power to carry out their mission to the world, then a better future for Europe should be realized.

CHAPTER II

The Role of the Church in War-time

(A Letter to American Christians)

DEAR FRIEND:

You and several other Christians in the United States have asked me (independently of one another) to write to America a letter of similar content to those which I have directed to France and England during the last few years. The somewhat presumptuous character of letters of this sort, and also the responsibility I take through them, is very obvious. After all, I am not seated in an apostolic chair which would formally bestow upon me the duty or the right to send out such epistles now and again!

Moreover, I have experienced how easy it is to be misunderstood in a milieu for the most part foreign, and in view of the enforced brevity of such utterances. I confess, for instance, that I am somewhat anxious at the thought of certain journalists who habitually pass by the really important content and by preference quote a few all too readily understood catchwords, peddling them about as my message, under the title "Dr. Barth says—." Now the United States in particular is so big, so remote from here,—not only geographically, and so little known to me inwardly, that I hesitated more than ever before.

On the other hand, I realize that the need for mutual understanding and strengthening grows more and more urgent, and as my American friends place some confidence in me, I shall try to come up to their expectations. You, dear friend, have come to my aid by laying before me a number of specific

19

questions, answers to which you consider especially important for the Christians of America. I shall try, then, as far and as well as I can, to take a stand in regard to those questions.

Permit me, to begin with, to state a general idea. I am glad to extract this from the questions you, as one who knows your Christian countrymen, have formulated: the gravity of the present world situation and its significance for the Christian and the ecclesiastical conscience are now in the process of being realized in the United States as well as here. All your questions show that the period of general incomprehension of the cause and inevitability of the present war, and also the period of that peculiar Christian indifference, impartiality, and lack of responsibility toward its problems and decisions, belong to the past.

I stress this because you can hardly imagine our embarrassment and trouble of mind during the long years when we watched the National Socialist tide in Germany rise higher and yet higher, but were compelled to note among other nations and people—and for so long a time in America, too—a certain superficial sensational interest. So far as the increasing danger as a whole was concerned, its nature and extent, there was only the most delightful complacency, the strongest possible determination not to see the danger, not to have to meet it under any circumstances. In Christian church circles, too, one hardly ever stumbled upon anything but the tedious manifestoes of an abstract moralism, which did indeed cross itself over certain exciting news from Germany, but without recognizing in the least the basic threat which was arising there, an attitude which too righteously and therefore unrighteously, shrank from and warned against all compromising commitments, continuously preaching peace where there neither was nor could be peace, and never noticing *whose* interests were being furthered thereby. This attitude certainly contributed not a little toward lulling the nations into the sleep from which they were later to be so tragically awakened.

Thus the most terrible day in recent years, for me and for

20

a few others, was not the defeat of France in 1940, nor the conquest of Crete in 1941, nor the event of Pearl Harbor, but that day in Munich in 1938 on which the nations that were responsible for the Peace of Versailles, by their betrayal of Czechoslovakia were forced to admit their impotence to uphold the order they had instituted in 1919; a day on which the Christian churches in all Europe rang their bells and felt themselves obligated to thank God for the avoidance of war brought about by that disgraceful pact. If I recall rightly, there was general contentment even in America—in Christian America—with what happened in Munich. The individual who was not satisfied, be he Winston Churchill or one of the few who, like him, stood with the opposition by reason of Christian concepts, could hardly hope for a hearing, but might well expect to fall into disrepute as a *provocateur* and war-monger.

Were there not at that time in the Western democracies, and even in their churches, all sorts of secret or even open admirers or at least defenders of Hitler? Were we not on the verge of carrying halfway to our lips (smiling sourly perhaps, but with a fatalistic sense of joy) the proffered cup filled with the poisonous and stupefying brew of the new ideal of humanity? It was then that I trembled—not before Hitler, but before the blindness of the uncounted multitude that, without really being *pro*-Hitler, nevertheless could not bring themselves to be actively *against* him.

You understand, dear friend, why I breathe easier today because of your questions, even though the intellectual and spiritual situation is still obscure enough. After all, it was not God's will that the world should remain in that unawareness of the obvious facts and thus run into the abyss which had opened before it. And above all, God did not suffer Christendom to continue the unfruitful moral reverie in which it could devise no way of opposing the complete explosion of a convinced and aggressive Godlessness save the spineless patter of a will-to-compromise and a pacifism which had long since become unChristian.

A certain awakening has taken place ; it remains for us to rub the last traces of sleep out of our eyes and, to avoid a relapse, to make quite clear to ourselves now what it means to be really awake. Certain decisions which are spiritual as well as political have been taken: the only thing that must still be done is to take them into clear, clean-cut and hence forceful and lasting decisions for us Christians. That is the salutary transformation of the situation which becomes visible to me from your questions and which makes it easier for me to write you now than if a similar assignment had come to me, say, four or five years ago. You must forgive me, however, if you should observe that the terror of those past days is still in my limbs. At that time I went through an anxiety which, in common with so many others, you probably did not feel to the same degree.

Your first question was:

How can a Christian be, at the same time, a loyal citizen of a national state and a loyal member of the Church Universal, which transcends national interests?

I think that as a Christian one must keep in mind first of all that it is not the essential nature of the State that it should be purely national, i. e., limited to a specific land and people and serving only national interests. That is the concept of the State which won through in the nineteenth century. But it was not the concept of the Middle Ages nor of the Roman Empire and Law. And above all, not that of the Bible. How could God prefer just *one*—this or that—national state, rather than first and foremost *his own,* the *true* State, within *all* national states?

Is not the function of government within the sovereignty of all nations and races (inclusive of the "state" form which may exist in any independent African tribe, or even in a robber's cave!) essentially the same: *the establishment and maintenance of an order of relationship between common rights*

22

and personal freedom, or rather, *responsibility?* Has there ever been a national state which, through international agreements with other states, could forego placing itself on the level of this common and obviously superior state-concept? That today the state practically exists only in a plurality of national states is only a historical and therefore variable fact, not an intrinsic and unalterable one. For example: once upon a time it was altogether different in Europe and it can again be altogether different, in Europe and in the rest of the world. Perhaps we must realize from the present war at least the clear insight that in this connection many changes must sooner or later take place.

So long as this has not occurred, the Christian will not fail to recognize and respect in the national state in which he lives, the essential, the internationally valid order of the true state instituted by God in his patience. Between the universal Church and the true state no essential or inevitable antithesis can exist, since after all both have been instituted by God, though with differing purpose. Nor can there be such contradiction between the universal Church and the national State in so far as the latter, *in its sphere* is in itself that essentially international, God-instituted *true* State. The Christian, therefore, can very well be, as a matter of principle, a loyal citizen of a National State (for instance: you a good American and I a good Swiss) *and* a loyal member of the universal Church. In fact, as long as there are only national states, he has no other choice than to direct to his national state the obedience and coöperation which he owes to the righteous state. He would not be giving to God that which is God's if he thought himself too good to give to Caesar (i. e., the National State) that which is Caesar's.

But—he will do the latter, however, in this way, that he will stand consistently for the universal, all-uniting order of the righteous state, even while giving full recognition to the rightly understood interests of the national state in which he lives. Thereby he will seek and further the best interests of his national state likewise. He will be on the watch for and if necessary protest against and resist everything in his national state which is incompatible with its character as the true state. He will, to the best of his ability, do his part to perfect and keep the national state as a righteous state. He will of course always be found among those who champion the effort to place international relations more and more completely on a basis on which national states can stand together as true states. A totally national state which serves *only* national interests—and we can see today that at least approximations of such a caricature are possible—would thereby *ipso facto* cease to be a righteous state. In this unrighteous state the Christian can show his civic loyalty only by resistance and suffering. Let us be thankful, you as an American, I as a Swiss, that this conflict in which our brethren in Germany, for instance, find themselves, has been spared us at least to this extent, that our national states, with all their imperfections, can nevertheless be classed to a fair degree as "righteous" states. Let us use this fact to the utmost advantage! We shall have our hands full.

Your second question:

Is this war to be conceived as the judgment of God on mankind? And if so, is there no distinction to be made between the more guilty and the less guilty?

Yes, I firmly believe that this war, like every other war, is a particularly visible form of the judgment of God on mankind. In times of peace the exercise of police power and the pronouncement and carrying out of sentence to maintain public order are unavoidable, but, even so, they are an indication of the divine judgment on human society. The same thing holds when two or more national states find no other way of ordering their relations to one another and of adjusting their national interests than through force of arms. The same thing holds even when, as is the case in the present war, the righteous state must be defended by force of arms against the explosion of anarchy and tyranny.

The necessity for the application of the *ultima ratio,* after all, invariably indicates many preceding wrongs and mistakes, and surely they are never all on one side. Human sin, the rebellion of man against his God, has then once more reached a stage where, when the state unsheathes the sword which, according to Romans 13, it does not bear in vain, a terrible sign of the wrath of God must become unmistakably apparent. It will then be wise—even in regard to the present war—to admit to oneself that over against this judgment of God there are no degrees of guilt. Who will measure the amount of culpability?

It can and must be said that *this* group of states (the United Nations today) has on the whole remained more righteous than *that* one (the Axis coalition). It can and should be said further, that this time the direct responsibility for the outbreak of war lies unequivocally on one side, namely, the side of Hitler and of the German people, unhappily blindly loyal and obedient to him. It is impossible to say, however, that in the whole tangled preliminary history of this war (to say nothing at all of the judgment of God) there should be some who are more, others who are less, guilty. Can Hitler be more guilty in the judgment of God than the men who in 1919 could write no better peace terms than those of Versailles? And by better I mean both more merciful *and* more stringent. Or was he more guilty than those who from 1919 to 1933 ran European politics neither with honest idealism nor with honest realism but simply without using their heads? Or more guilty than the pacifists (both by principle and utilitarianism) who contributed so much to make the world defenseless over against the surprise of 1933?

Was "the man on the street" of Berlin or Munich, with his errors and stupidities, guiltier than his comrades in London, Paris, or New York with theirs? And one might continue: have the populations more cause to upbraid the governments than vice-versa?—the workers the rich, or the rich the workers—the Jews to accuse the anti-Semites or the other way around? Has the Church a better case against society than the latter has against the Church?

It will be appropriate and necessary to analyze and to admit specifically the mistakes made on all sides. It will also be inevitable that those who are directly responsible for the present catastrophe as such will have to suffer for the disaster they have caused. But it could only lead to endless bickering if we were to reckon up and throw in each other's faces who was more, who was less responsible for the fact that we must today experience in war the judgment of God for humanity and if we were to hold Hitler and the German people, as it were, metaphysically and theologically accountable for it. (That which awaits them is bad enough without this last). And the right, well-thought-out and effective conduct of the war would only be hindered. For the war cannot be fought on any other presupposition than that we human beings have no faults to reckon up against one another before God, but only to forgive them to one another.

Very definitely, the war is not an instrument of the divine vengeance against one or the other; even police power and the processes of justice cannot be that in time of peace: "Vengeance is mine, saith the Lord—" War is rather and quite simply the dreadful ultimate instrument for the restoration of the public order, broken and destroyed by mutual guilt. The fact that there is in war an "enemy"—today his name is Hitler, and alas, also Germany—means simply that the disease from which we have all suffered broke out in that spot and can only be cured by an operation in that place. So much Nihilism in all sorts of forms had already accumulated throughout the entire world that at last it had to reach an explosion point in Hitler's tyranny and anarchy: that is the lesson we must learn from this war, and that shows us the attitude we must take toward it.

The more readily we realize and admit that we all stand equally under God's judgment in this war; that this war in itself can assume the character of a serious "police action" which, while bringing unavoidable suffering to all, may be a defense of the "righteous" state—and the less we (who are all in similar need of God's forgiveness) concentrate the war effort on any single guilty person or nation—the more cold-bloodedly and energetically will the war be waged, for then, and only then, can we have a good conscience in this hard and terrible business. As a serious, orderly police action, with the sober objective of destroying Hitler and rendering Germany and its allies harmless for all time to come, the war is in itself a beneficent, and despite all its harshness and terror, a merciful thing, which is in the truest interest of even those most directly affected thereby.

It would not have been good for Hitler himself if he had been allowed to run his course unhindered in 1939. It would not have been good for the German, the Italian or the Japanese people if the rest of the world had submitted to the senseless aspirations with which they entered the war. The war *against* them is in fact also being waged *for* them. But as the execution of the divine vengeance on the guilty, or at least the more guilty, it could not be a just undertaking. Nations and governments and armies would then be conducting it with hypocritical self-righteousness, with an uneasy conscience in view of their own share in the guilt, and the outcome of the war would in any case only provide the cause for new evils and subsequent new wars. If this is not what is wanted, then one must, for heaven's sake, refrain from imagining this to be a crusade of the just against the unjust, of the white against the black sheep.

I should like therefore to give to the first part of your question the answer that we must give heed to Romans 13: 1, 7; and to the second part of your question that we must place beside the above the words of Romans 3: 23, and in this relation realize the whole political as well as Christian truth.

Your third question:

What is the true function of the Church and its ministers in relation to this war? Should church bodies and pastors actively support the prosecution of the war by preaching about the issues involved, by urging the membership of the churches to serve in the armed forces, to buy war bonds, etc.? Or should they confine their activities to the timeless "spiritual" ministries? What are the limits beyond which the Church should not go in identifying itself with any political cause? In what sense is it true that the Church is not at war?

If I understand correctly, you are asking me first of all what the churches, i. e., the church bodies and their ministers, should or should not say and do in the present situation. I I should not like to evade the question, but I should like to point out that the first consideration is an entirely inward task of the Church. Is the Church clearly aware that its mission in every, and therefore also in this time, is solely (and this in the fullest sense of the concept!) *to preach the word of God to the mankind of today, according to the Holy Writ?* Has it accepted the events and problems of our time as an admonition to renew its awareness of the breadth of this mission in all its aspects? In other words, has the Church realized that the world catastrophe which has befallen us has a connection with a catastrophe of the Church, and that to face this fact is far more important and urgent than all the "yeas" and "nays" which the Church must preach to the outside, and that to face it is the prerequisite for every vigorous "yea" and "nay" directed to the outer world?

I should here like to take the liberty of proposing a counter-question: what is being done today in the church bodies, ministerial conferences, theological faculties, but above all in the studies of the individual pastors of all denominations in the United States, to the end that the Church shall again be the Church, understand itself as such and act accordingly? Did not the manifest unsureness of the churches on both sides of the Atlantic in recent years, in the light of the events of our time, stem to some degree from the fact

28

that nothing (or too little), had been done for the inward regeneration of the churches? You cannot gather grapes from thistles. It could not be expected that a club for the furtherance of religious humanism would have the discernment to recognize the National Socialist menace and find the correct warning voice to lift against it. And today we cannot expect that it would give the nations clear guidance in the great difficulties of their wartime problems and sufferings; that it would represent the Kingdom of Christ, and not enter the service of some earthly sovereignty. The narrow way of cleancut decision and complete freedom is trod only by the Church that *is* the Church or is about to become the Church once more.

I do not know whether, and to what extent, such a Church again exists in America—we in Europe have scarcely taken more than the first steps in that direction—but if there is something comparable in the United States, I shall be all the better understood if I say that the true function of the Church consists first of all in its own regeneration: in a regeneration no less thorough than the Reformation through which Protestantism began in the sixteenth century. How do matters stand in your country in this respect? In sending this counterquestion, I should like to reply as follows to your third question:

1. If the Church is really preaching the *Word of God,* then this will mean active support of the war effort in so far as it testifies, with a clarity consistent with the Word of God, that the carrying through of this stern police action against Hitler's Nihilism is a necessary task of the righteous state; that therefore the United States has rightly embarked upon this task and that the American Christian is obligated to help his country, within the framework of his vocation and his abilities, in the accomplishment of this task.

Recently we read here in Switzerland a pronouncement by ninety-three leading American Protestants and we were informed that this was a statement characteristic of the majority of the American churches. In this statement is the sentence: "We abhor war, but upon the outcome of this war depends the realization of Christian principles to which no Christian can be indifferent." I venture to doubt that this is the unequivocal language, appropriate to God's word, which should be employed today. If the realization of Christian principles depends upon the outcome of this war, then there is no point in the assurance that war is abhorrent: for it is surely only unnecessary and unjust wars which are condemned as abhorrent, and among this number the present one is not to be classed. If, conversely, war as such is really condemned, then the realization of Christian principles must definitely not be made dependent on its outcome: that would mean the determination to do evil in violation of conscience, in order that good may result. I give this as an example of what I do *not* consider to be the true exercise of the pastoral function and true preaching in the present situation. The Word of God cannot be rightly preached in such equivocal sentences, and an adequate "active undergirding of the war effort" can likewise not be attained by such phrases.

2. If the Church really proclaims the Word of God according to Holy Writ, then there can be no reason for its making the war, its causes, problems, tasks and outlook, the theme of its preaching and for its making the obligation to military service and to buy war bonds and the like the contents of its exhortation. Holy Writ does not demand of the preachers of the Gospel (nor is it needed by the people of today any more than in all other ages) that they proclaim from the pulpit again what is already being sufficiently stated by the newspapers and the propaganda agencies of the State far better than the preachers could state it. Unhappy preachers, and above all, unhappy parishes, where that is the case.

What, then, shall they preach? The Word of the reconciliation of the world with God through Jesus Christ (2 Cor. 5: 17–21) and nothing else. But this in its full scope! When they preach about the sole sovereignty of Jesus Christ, His human origin among the people of Israel, His triumph over powers and dominations, about God's mercy and patience

30

revealed in Him, the dual benefaction of Church and State realized in Him; about the impossibility of serving two masters, about freedom, and the service of the children of God conceived in the Holy Spirit, they are inevitably preaching, through a simple, strict interpretation of the biblical texts, (and as a rule without naming persons and things specifically) against Hitler, Mussolini and Japan; against anti-Semitism, idolization of the State, oppressive and intimidating methods, militarism, against all the lies and the injustice of National Socialism and Fascism in its European and its Asiatic forms, and thus they will naturally (and without "dragging politics into the pulpit") speak on behalf of the righteous state and also for an honestly determined conduct of the war. And this procedure will also admirably take care of the necessary practical exhortation—usually without the need to refer to military service, war loans, and the like. Just at this time the message of Holy Writ is in itself strong and unequivocal enough to be comprehensible in a very pointed way, even to a child. We must simply make ourselves once more obedient to it, wholeheartedly, and rule out all secondary purposes.

3. When the Church is truly preaching the Word of God to the *man of today,* there can be no question of confining itself to a "timeless" spiritual service. What exactly is that, anyway? There is a "timeless" religion, a "timeless" standard of morals. The Word of God, however, is never "timeless." The time in which we live is the time accorded to us, through God's patience, between the resurrection of Jesus Christ and His second coming. Therefore it is God's time. Therefore He and His Word have a necessary, innate relation to everything that transpires within this time, and thus to the American man of today who sees himself in one way or another involved in the war against Germany, Italy and Japan.

What kind of sermon and what sort of ministry would it be whose consolation and admonition guided mankind to some timeless vacuum remote from the real conditions of this world with its anxieties and problems, or which led men to a sort of religious-moral "private" life? I wonder if the people in

America, who are now, it appears, sponsoring that type of preaching and ministry, are quite aware that they are thereby moving in the wake of a certain type of German Lutheranism which has been preaching for centuries that the Gospel and the Law, the transcendent and the terrestrial, the Church and the State, Christian and political living, may be regarded and treated as two neatly separated realms. Do they realize the extent to which this evil doctrine furthered the German nationalism, *étatisme* and militarism of the nineteenth century and finally the National Socialism of today? If the Church in America has a craving for smoothing the road in that country for the rise of a similar secularistic monster, a diligent regimen of "timeless" spiritual ministry is highly to be recommended: no slogan is more pleasing to the devil than this one! If such is not their desire, churchmen must bear in mind that for some reason it pleased the Word of God to become finite and therefore also law-bound, imminent and political in the person of Jesus Christ, not only without detracting from His character as Gospel, as hope of resurrection, as the utterance of the Church, but rather in confirmation and fulfillment thereof.

Leave to the Word its whole independence and dignity by preaching it according to Holy Writ! But leave to it also, on the other hand, its full strength and scope, by not forgetting for a moment to preach it to the man of today as such and therefore also in its whole finite and political clarity and categorical firmness.

4. Identification of the Church with a political cause? No! Under no circumstances and not even within the most modest limits! That is not the idea at all, that the Church identify itself—even remotely—with any political cause, that of the Allies, for instance, and so provide the religious accompaniment to the terrible sounds which must now travel round the world. By doing so it would betray its Lord and surrender itself without rendering the cause of the Allies the least assistance. A single true man with an ordinary gun in his hand would be more useful to the Allies' cause than the bells and

32

organs of all the churches in the world if they, having betrayed their Master and thereby surrendered themselves, were no longer "true" churches. In complete independence (of the Allied cause as well) they can and should be a light to their members and to the entire world, a light making visible the fact that the terrible calamity of our day is no blind accident, no mere expression of general human benightedness, no senseless free-for-all between different imperialistic systems; that it would not do any good to turn away from it in indignation and divert one's thoughts because it is so "horrible" and to escape from it and leave to others the responsibility for seeing it through.

The churches can and should make it plain that Jesus Christ is now, as always, Lord of the world and all its dominions and that today's world-rending struggle also is being fought (whether mankind realizes and admits it or not) for His sake and in honor of Him, and has His Promise, so that those who know and love Him must, before all others, take this war seriously. Or is there not some danger that the meaning of this war may be misconstrued, and become simply futile, insane, and abhorrent? How could it be otherwise? Human life is always threatened by this possibility. The noblest cause is not immune from becoming an evil one in our hands, and if this war is a good cause, it is nevertheless a dangerous one, a temptation for all the participating nations, governments, and armies.

Woe betide, if the Church should desecrate itself in this cause instead of seeing to it, on the contrary, that this cause be consecrated through the Church, that the righteousness and necessity of this war for the defense of the righteous state be preserved to the nations, to their governments and armies *consciously,* thus giving them a clear conscience in the conduct of it but also preserving the moderation necessary to its proper conclusion. This mission, by virtue of which it preaches a righteous peace in the midst of war and thus approves the war only for the sake of the righteous peace (but for its sake does so in wholehearted earnest), is the prophetic

33

mission of the Church in this war. And if it is only Church, and remains Church, it cannot be estimated to what extent it may impose limitation on itself in its realization of this mission. Its spiritual mission in this respect is illimitable. Let the Church take care, however, that it be and remain strictly true to it as to its spiritual mission!

5. The sentence, that the Church is not at war, is *true to the extent* that it may mean: the Church is in no sense one of the instruments of the warring state. In war as in peace it serves its own Lord, pursues its own cause and speaks its own language: the cause and message of the Gospel, which is directed to friend and foe alike and is not dependent on the outcome of the war, whatever it may be. It prays, while admonishing the friendly powers to remain absolutely steadfast, for the Church and for the enemy. It always remains determined and ready to intercede, if necessary, for the rights of the enemy also.

The same sentence is *in part not true,* in so far as it can mean: the Church is neutral, it looks on and takes care not to compromise itself. It preaches a Gospel which is indifferent to the question of a righteous state, motivated by no clear political decisions and objectives. It might even disseminate the lie that recognition between left and right, between good and evil in this war is not required. It confines its activities to that timeless spiritual service, etc., etc.

That same sentence is *wholly true* in so far as it means: the Church in wartime lives and works—to the very degree that it takes the war seriously—in the deepest peace of the knowledge that He, who makes all things new, is already seated victoriously at the right hand of God; the King, whose sovereignty has no end, who needs no service from us but who has not scorned the enlistment on His behalf of our earnest, determined, persistent service in Church and State.

CHAPTER III

The Church and Post-War Reconstruction

Your fourth question:

How far should the churches go in formulating concrete plans for a better political and economic order in Europe—and in the world—after the war? Should they, for example, insist in the name of Christianity on the formation of a federated Europe (and possibly of a world federation) in which national sovereignty is transcended?

These questions and all the subsequent ones concern the *Future after the War.* Permit me first to ask again a general counter-question:

I always find it hard not to become restless, yes, even impatient, when I hear my English and American friends talk and argue so much about the war aims and about all sorts of problems and objectives for the days after the war. The process reminds me uncannily of the German emigrants in Paris, London, New York and elsewhere in 1933, all constantly preoccupied with the new constitution and ordering of the German Reich with which they intended to dower their homeland after Hitler's fall. I cannot get over the disproportion between these worries for the future and the present reality. The desperation, suffering, bleeding, dying. In the occupied countries a dogged opposition defies the German execution orders, but hunger and moral disintegration of all sorts are threatening more and more to get the upper hand. Even the modest task of preserving Switzerland as an island of order and humanity takes our whole strength, from month to month.

35

Over in America, however, dear friend, there still seem to be wide circles who have enough superfluous time and energy to speculate with great fervor about how to divide the bear's skin—after everything which must be done to kill him has been carried out successfully! Here I stand before a riddle which for the present I cannot solve along human, political, or theological lines.

It goes without saying that we all try to form some sort of concepts of the post-war world. I should like, however, to ask —and I am entirely willing to be enlightened—what is to be gained from the process of putting these imaginative concepts, in the form of a miniature eschatology, so far into the foreground of your reflections as is evidenced in your questions? Do you think that the anxieties and problems of today can be better overcome if you constantly dream of tomorrow? Or do you expect to tackle the anxieties and problems of tomorrow all the better because you are speculating today about plans which you think will guide you tomorrow?

Aren't you the least bit disturbed by the trivial realization that obviously it is necessary *now, now, now*—and if it is impossible now, then at least *very soon*—to act, help, fight with might and main, because the future may depend on what is done now (or very soon)—or is left undone? To give due attention to another point of view: wouldn't it be better form not to open these discussions of the future at least until the Allied troops are really at the Rhine, or better, beyond the Rhine, or have the great decisive effort successfully behind them, one way or another; that great effort for which they have prepared for so long and of which they have talked so much. And doesn't this likewise insignificant truth bother you, that human affairs, big and little—very likely because they are in God's hands—with a certain degree of regularity take some other totally different course from that which was foreseen at the start, and that the plans for the future, as constructed today, quite as regularly reveal themselves as so much love's labor lost, largely because the most important facts of the future when they actually occur usually come upon us so unexpectedly that a liquidation of the previously made reckoning is almost inevitable? Are we living today according to the plans we hatched out four or five years ago? How can we hope to live in another three to five years on what we are trying so hard to work out now? Doesn't your Bible, too, contain the command not to take thought for tomorrow because sufficient to the day are the evils thereof? And the story of the Israelites in the desert who every day received the celestial food which they needed for that day, whereas this same food spoiled when they wanted to keep a supply for the next day?

Isn't this true: if the churches would today bend all their efforts to become once more true to their real mission, and change from well-meaning religious organizations back into real churches—if, engaged in this act of repentance and renewal, they would seek, find and probably effectively preach *today*, the right, clear, joyful message pertinent to the anxieties and problems of *today*, including the burdens imposed on the world of fighting the war—that would be the real, sound, prophetic preparation for their mission of tomorrow, that tomorrow-after-the-war, whatever the outcome of the war may be in specific cases and whatever special tasks may then be waiting for the churches. Actually, what do the churches need to know in advance for that future, other than that their Lord will be with them then (Matthew 28: 20) and that everything will then depend on this: that they be ready and willing in His service? And what can they do for that future save this: that now, in this present during which they are nearing that future, they may be truly obedient to their mission? "Today, while ye hear His voice." (Heb. 3: 7)

And this also is true: if the *state,* on its part, turns its energies *today* thoroughly and far-sightedly to its multiple war problems, and thus proves and maintains itself as a righteous state; if in the political, military, economic, social and cultural fields it does *now* what it must do for the effective removal of the evil now threatening us, if its procedure *today* is a proof of sober and determined execution of its special mission, then that is not only the best, but the only realistic preparation for the end of the war and for peace, with the problems and duties which will then be waiting.

When Churchill and Roosevelt, in the famous Atlantic Charter, gave us a little sketch of their ideas about the time after the war, that was very satisfactory, and the likelihood that there probably exists in all governments some subdivision in which all kinds of concrete post-war plans are being made ready for this or that eventuality, is, from a practical point of view, even more satisfactory. But wasn't there at one time something or other such as the fourteen points of President Wilson? Can a sensible individual doubt that the Atlantic Charter is more interesting in the light of certain propaganda needs of today (perhaps already of yesterday) than for the real future, about which Churchill and Roosevelt share our dreams and reflections but over which they have no power? I am sure they would be the first to admit this. And if really good work is done in those subdivisions for post-war plans, in what can it consist save in the orientation of certain viewpoints for very divergent *eventualities* which however may, at the decisive moment, be superseded by entirely new and unexpected eventualities, compelling the governments to make quite other orientations?

Whatever can be done for the future on the part of the state (and by all of us in our role as citizens)—*done,* not just talked about!—must be done in and for the present or it won't be done at all. If it *is* done—if we *do* it (as Christians in the joyous certainty that our future, like our present, belongs not to us but to God), then we may well leave it to the future to *show whether* at the end of the war and in peacetime, we will not be equal to assuming the tasks awaiting us in some other form.

I beg your pardon if I felt compelled to be so explicit in the formulation of my counter-question. I did it because I have the impression that on this matter I am talking to my American friends through a particularly thick wall, and because I believe the existence of this wall to be a mighty dangerous business. Did I not labor this point sufficiently in my letter to

England which was read widely and carefully in America? If I could only shake this wall a little: this wall which seems to me to consist of a dangerously unworldly "futurism"—or if I could be convinced that it is really, in the human, political and Christian sense, that good and essential cause for which you obviously take it, and which I cannot for the time being see in that light at all!

The Christian concept of the righteous state, which is endorsed now and always by the churches, undoubtedly has a distinct *limitation* and a *distinct* orientation. Since it aims at *order,* the righteous state contradicts and withstands all political, social, and economic tyranny and anarchy. And since it makes the rights of the community *and* personal responsibility the yardstick of order, *democracy* comes nearer to that ideal state than an aristocratic or monarchical dictatorship, *socialism* than an untrammeled capitalistic order with the social and business system based on it; a *federation of free states* (free also as much as possible from the principle of nationalism) than the rivalry of independent and uncontrolledly competing national states. Therefore there could and can be only one stand for the churches to take in the present conflict.

And this consideration might well decide the initiation and the general trend of your post-war attitude toward peacetime problems. It must not be forgotten, however: the Christian concept of the righteous state does indeed embrace the absolute requirement of order, justice and freedom, but no absolute demand regarding the molding of public life into this or that form of government which is possible on this basis. When we remember that Romans 13: 1–7 was written under the shadow of the Roman state at the time of Nero, we cannot say that democracy, or socialism, or a narrower or wider circle of federated states must be an essential, permanent and universal Christian postulate, to be maintained under all circumstances; and conversely that dictatorship, an unhindered type of independent national states, must necessarily be condemned as unchristian and fought as such. Order, justice,

39

and freedom *can* be frustrated even under those *better* forms of government, and they *can* be honored even under the worse forms.

It is an absolute Christian requirement that this last—the preservation of order, justice and freedom—be upheld under all conditions, and not the introduction of the better, or the removal of the worse form of public administration. The churches will always have to guide by this distinction. They will have to point in that *direction* and call attention to that limitation (always in accord with their mission to preach the living Word of God), when the inevitable world-wide post-war regeneration is actually present and ready for real discussion. They will then, we hope, unequivocally champion that which is indubitably right. But we hope also that they will take good care not to identify themselves with some specific state or social philosophy, nor to act as if they themselves had a "Christian" state and social philosophy to represent and sponsor, as if this were that "essential" which they were to preach. In obedience to the living, divine Word, but also with due attention to the practical conditions and presuppositions of the necessary regeneration, they will then have to say what must be said in this matter and it will then be decided in what *form* they will endorse an "order," to what *degree* and in what *sense* they will support the democratic, socialistic, and federative establishment of right and freedom.

How could the churches start investigations *now* about the specific content of their future message, their demands, and perhaps even their protest, or enter into agreements and issue information about them? The Word of God tomorrow will surely not be a mere repetition of what, with the best knowledge and intent, we believe we hear today. And what do we know today about the practical conditions and presuppositions under which we shall then have to preach the Word of God? What do we know about the form in which Soviet Russia will emerge from this war and what we ought, and what we ought not, to learn from it then? What do we know of the manner in which Germany will experience and accept its defeat, and of the way in which the upheaval there will be accomplished? Or of the forces which have now brought the United States and Britain together, and which may also lead them apart? Or of the factors which China and perhaps India, too, will introduce at that moment? Or of the frame of mind in which the middle class and the labor element in the warring and neutral countries, the oppressed masses in the occupied countries and the not less oppressed masses in Germany, Italy, and Japan will come out of the present crisis?

What do we know about the personalities who will then be at the helm hither and yon and sit at the conference tables? (We know well enough the role played by personalities in the shaping of the Peace of 1919!) Or about the question as to whether on that day we will have to reckon with a certain useful political enthusiasm or with a widespread paralyzing fatigue? (After 1918 all the world wanted to do was dance!)

I ask you: in the face of so many most important and as yet unpredictable factors, how shall we make concrete plans and decisions as to what form, in what degree and sense the Christian concept of the state is to be validated? How much will then be possible or necessary whereof we cannot even dream today? And how much of what we now reckon among the surest inventory of our expectations for the future will then perhaps be quite impossible and wholly useless? Do we really need to know now what we are going to say then? According to Matthew 10: 11, 12, is it not indicative of lack of faith to want to know all that today? Haven't we something better to do? I fear that if we have nothing better to do, then we may at the decisive moment stand there again, with our concrete plans in our heads and our pockets, without counsel or guidance for ourselves or for others.

Your fifth question:

Should the American churches try to persuade the American

41

people and the American government to accept a responsibility for enforcing order and peace, by the use of armed force, after the war? If they do so, how can they avoid the rise of an American "imperialism"?

Whether it will be necessary for the American government not only to restore peace by armed force *during* war, but also to *help maintain* it after the war, is something we don't know at present. If it proves to be necessary, I cannot see how the American government can do half a job, that is, perform the first part of the task and neglect the other. All governments have, we hope, learned from the failure of the Peace of Versailles that if world politics is to make sense, he who says: "A" must also say: "B, C and D"—in other words, follow through. It seems obvious to me that if the American government should, contrary to expectations, fall down in this respect, the American churches would have the duty to petition their government to act in this instance as a righteous state should. The peace after this war must be one that is guaranteed by every human means, otherwise it will have been fought in vain.

Now, however, you manifestly fear an American "imperialism" in this connection. Well, of course we may well fear that all sorts of new and perhaps worse forms of imperialism may arise as a result of this war. (Soviet Russia!) Natural man is an evil brute, one who is always glad of a chance to start over again, under another disguise, the game once lost. But you see it is never wise to allow oneself to be delayed or diverted from the right path by the possibility of all sorts of dangers which might develop sooner or later. The danger of an American imperialism is no evidence against the fact that America must go ahead on the road it has entered and finish the job. Otherwise all has been in vain! Try to convince every American of this, it is the best thing you can do to avert that danger if it should threaten. An American imperialism was dangerous at the time when America, following evil nationalistic examples, wished to concern itself only with its own affairs. If it remains true to the world political mission which it

42

has undertaken, it will of itself *not* become imperialistic. I cannot see how the American churches could do anything better than to come out strongly for your nation remaining true to that international mission. If this is not done for some reason and the danger becomes acute, *then* one might have to challenge the churches and nations to oppose America as they are now being called upon to oppose Hitler. Don't doubt for a moment that in such a case I should certainly not remain silent! But why should you and I amuse ourselves by painting such devils on the wall?

Your sixth question:

What policies should the American churches support with reference to relations with (a) Germany, (b) Russia, after the war?

Here I admit that I am in some embarrassment concerning your eschatological interest. We don't know what (a) Germany, (b) Russia, will be after the war. How can we judge what policy toward them will be the most suitable, which will then be the one which should receive support from the American churches? We only know (a) that the German army is not beaten and (b) that it is Russia which has to date achieved the most effective action against Germany and which has made the heaviest sacrifices. I cannot urge these positive contemporary facts too strongly upon your attention.

And I venture only to voice a general thought with a view to Germany, which I have especially at heart, and which I *suppose* will have to be taken up seriously, namely: when (or if) the German menace (even perhaps a future menace) is somehow completely ended, if at the same time a real service is to be rendered to the constituent German nations and people, then we shall have to dare to understand the Germans better than they understand themselves and thus nullify the unfortunate work of Bismarck—the worst of the nationalistic errors of the nineteenth century. We shall have to restore

43

their local sovereignty to the different German states—Austria, Bavaria, Wurttemberg, Saxony, Hanover, Hessia, etc.—to a degree and in a sense still to be determined. The "German Reich" rests on a misapprehension which has worked out ill not only for other peoples and nations but above all for Germany itself.

Let the German tribes politically be once more what they really are and have never ceased to be despite Bismarck and Hitler. See to it that they can support themselves economically but help them to waken from the terrible dream of being "a great power"—a dream which is terrible for them even more than for others—and enable them to live their own life in the community of other nations and so be really true to their mission! After the war they will need many unselfish, attentive and patient friends. There never was a people so sick as the German people today. It will surely be in a more pitiable state tomorrow than all those upon which it has brought so much distress. It will only be possible to help them, however (in so far as human aid from without is possible at all), if the hand that is offered to them is a very firm one. The task will be gigantic. But I hasten to add that this question, too, may bear an entirely different aspect when the war is over, and I should therefore like to consider the thoughts sketched above as given "off the record."

Your seventh question:

What spiritual qualifications are essential in American Christians who desire to be helpful to the European churches in the period of reconstruction following the war?

Here, too, I experience a certain embarrassment. After the war we shall certainly be grateful to every American Christian who undertakes to be helpful to the European churches in the post-war period of reconstruction. Answering the question as to what qualities are essential on the part of such an

44

American, would, however, depend on what is meant by (a) "spiritual qualities" and (b) by "helpful." If the question is strictly of a New Testament nature, the only answer is: such an American will come to us as bearer of the whole apostolic Gospel of Jesus Christ and must be helpful to our churches by showing them in his person and by his utterance how they can better be churches and believe, hope and hence be a better light to this dark world than heretofore. But perhaps the question is less strictly meant. Perhaps you wish the word "spiritual" to be understood more in the sense of "intellectual." In that case I should like to give a double reply:

1. Such an American must be well acquainted with the European churches he wants to help before he gets here. He must not have learned about them too quickly nor too much along the lines of ready-made slogans. He should have given serious study and made himself reasonably familiar with their history, their external, and internal situations, their problems and difficulties, their insights and strength. I should like to add as an urgent wish: he must know our language a bit, be able to read our books and papers himself, if necessary, to follow our worship services and other gatherings with some understanding and perhaps be able to speak with us a little in our own tongue.

2. This American must come equipped with a better, not with a less adequate, theology than is usual over here. He must be more firmly grounded in the Christian faith, be a better student of the Bible, a better preacher, pastor and ecclesiastical statesman, and as such have greater gravity and also a keener sense of humor than the average European theologian. The latter have many and serious faults: these must not be confirmed by the American emissary! They have some good points, in these they must not surpass the American but must be surpassed by him.

You see, dear friend, that it will be pretty difficult for America to be helpful to the European churches. Not because they are particularly exacting, but because they are particularly needy and after the war will be more so. The finest intellec-

45

tual and spiritual qualities of that helpful American will be just good enough to render effective aid. I should not be taking your question seriously if I answered in any other way. But you can see that, here, too, my answer points to the present—everything depends on what qualities the American churches acquire today in order to be helpful to others.

And now permit me to put another question and state another wish as *addendum* to your last question: I know that the American churches take a great and praiseworthy interest in the Ecumenical Movement, whose Council, or Bureau, has its headquarters here in Geneva. And I believe that the development and setting in motion of this organization is one of the things through which you will not be averse to helping the Europe and the world of the post-war period.

During the last few years I have had frequent reason to deplore the fact that while all sorts of useful data were gathered in Geneva, reports were issued, all kinds of preliminary studies engaged in, all sorts of visiting and correspondence were furthered and technical aid given and occasionally (but more in a personal way) certain advice was relayed to the suffering churches under fire, still at no time was Geneva, and thus the Ecumenical Movement, *heard* in this decisive moment of the history of these times. Not in 1933 (the start of the German church struggle), nor in the summer and fall of 1938, when the political storm was gathering, nor in 1939, when it broke loose, neither at the time of the catastrophe of 1940 nor since then, was there directed to Christendom and to mankind a witnessing, clarifying, encouraging and comforting word from the ecumenical center. Why did I and do I have to send out such letters simply as a private individual after all the beautiful words which have been spoken and written again and again about the new unity of the Church of Jesus Christ discovered in the Ecumenical Movement? Why did "Geneva" always leave it to me to speak out? Why did you—though *via* Geneva it is true—direct your questions to me and not to the Geneva center itself? I mean: why is the "one" church not in the arena with its message when such

46

questions as yours are being discussed in the various churches? Why do they have to look to a professor, who, as such, can offer only his individual utterance and is from the outset impeded by the knowledge that what he says will be accepted and treated simply as his private opinion?

In answer to all these questions with which I have plagued our mutual friend in Geneva often enough, I was always told that the Ecumenical Council or Bureau had no authority, no commission, and no power to speak publicly and authoritatively in the way I requested. I heard again and again that the whole institution was just "in process of formation" and thus to some extent incapable of taking action. Permit me again to become a little excited: is it not truly deplorable that the only organ in the world in which the Ecumenical Movement and the "rediscovered church of Christ" were not merely the subject of fine speeches, but which had attained a modest, yet discernible form in the shape of a tiny staff of selected and qualified men and women, that this center was not yet ready to act during *these* years, but was engaged in some endless process of development in which state it was obviously expected to remain for the time being? Is it not almost tragi-comic that conferences are held there and much doubtless valuable testimony is gathered on the *theme*, "The Message of the Church to the World" but that one doesn't dare even to think of the conception and publication to the world of *real* messages of the *Church*—always still "in process of formation"?

What are they waiting for? I have hitherto aimed this question at our friend in Geneva but realize that I ought to put it to "Geneva" instead, with a view to hastening this "process" a bit and thus giving the Geneva organ in some way the authority, the assignment, the power, so that it may be enabled really to be the Ecumenical *Council* and thus be able not merely to take counsel but also to give it with real weight, as it is most certainly needed by the churches in Europe and all the world. Don't tell me that a thing like the publicly binding utterance of a real Council of the Churches united in the

47

Ecumenical Movement must necessarily have the character of a papal encyclical and that the union of those churches has not progressed sufficiently for such action? Isn't there such a thing as a frank and binding fraternal word, spoken in apostolic freedom, and shouldn't the genuineness of the rediscovered intellectual oneness of the Church of Christ—in contrast to the papal unity of the false church which we certainly shall not strive to emulate—be made manifest when such free, apostolic, brotherly words are spoken in its name?

I ask: why are they delaying in the churches of the world to confirm the Geneva organ in some way (perhaps under present circumstances more in the organizational sense than in that of content) so that mere study and discussion may be replaced by *Christian utterance* and *Christian action?* Don't they see that the Ecumenical Movement and the Ecumenical Council, if they are not capable of this, will be viewed in history as a friendly but impotent game like the League of Nations of 1919, which likewise became morally bankrupt because nobody felt inclined to accept the responsibility for endowing it with *power?* What the Ecumenical Movement and the Ecumenical Council need is *ecclesiastical power.* Our friends in Geneva maintain that they do not have it since the churches of the world do not back them up with an expressly assigned mission and declaration of confidence. I am of a different opinion: they should long ago, without asking leave, have given proof of spirit and strength even at the risk of being blamed for it in some places.

But I realize that they really need such definite expression of confidence and authorization. And so I implore: let it be given to them! I hope they are not futuristically awaiting the *eschaton* of the end of the war and the hypothetical possibilities which might then have to be considered? No! *Now* is the time when the One Church should be heard in the churches and thereby become a living reality. How can it do so later if it does not and will not venture to be heard now? May I not summon the American churches—which I address through you—that alone or together with the churches of other lands,

48

they take *at once* the steps appropriate to make this transformation *now?* In this the American churches would be immediately helpful to the European churches without awaiting the proposed reconstruction period.

With this I close this letter which has grown unduly long. I know that you will receive it in friendship and understanding in all its particulars. Greet all those who, with you, are concerned about the questions concerning which I have here spoken my thoughts. God be with you, and with us over here.

In Christian fellowship, yours

KARL BARTH

Basle
December 12, 1942